Stewardship As A Lifestyle

Seeking to live as a Steward and Disciple

By

Dr. John R. Frank, CFRE

www.DesignGroupInternational.com

Dog Ear Publishing
4010 W. 86th Street, Ste H
Indianapolis, IN 46268
www.dogearpublishing.net

ISBN: 978-1-4575-1576-7

This book is printed on acid-free paper.

Printed in the United States of America

Table of Contents

Introduction

When I set out to write this book I was completing my doctoral work with a dissertation focused on stewardship education. After finishing, I was faced with the reality that not one of the theological schools or seminaries I sent my dissertation to had interest in the topic, the course, or a suggested curriculum for an MA in Stewardship and Development.

So the Lord began guiding me to this book. The best way to introduce a *new stewardship* would be by going to the leaders, followers, and readers of stewardship.

My hope is that all who read this book will see an encouraging and positive opportunity to embrace biblical stewardship in the church and our individual lives. Stewardship is a key issue for the life of a disciple and it brings positive results to the follower.

The first section of the book outlines my research and findings, offering a new look and consideration for stewardship. Hopefully readers will find some compelling and thought provoking ideas to bring stewardship back from simply fundraising to its important role in our relationship with God.

The second section contains short chapters with simple concepts for consideration. Each describes a stewardship focus with a few questions for you to use in a variety of settings. It may be a catalyst for a message from the pulpit, a small group study, or as a starting point for your church or personal discipleship training. These chapters are not exhaustive, but if this little book becomes a tool for discussion and additional research and reflection, then it will achieve a great purpose.

The movement to return biblical stewardship to the forefront of the church, and the individual lives of Jesus' disciples, is needed more than ever. When we all see our lives as a holistic relationship with a generous Creator we will truly impact this world for God's name and purpose. I pray this book is encouraging and challenging to the body of Christ.

SECTION ONE

*Understanding Stewardship
As A Disciple*

CHAPTER 1

Living a Lifestyle

Can someone tell us how to look at life? Most of us do it without thinking. We all look at life through our own filters. Filters are built or clogged with the experiences, teaching, and learning that we go through. The resulting issues, feelings, or opinions influence how we will live our lives. They also become additional filters by which we view life.

I believe the stewardship filter is clogged in the church, in the pastor, and in the follower of Jesus. Our lifestyle filter is filled up with tradition, ritual, preference, resentment, history, doctrine and denominational rules. This list is not wrong or evil. It is just that as we go through life, one person may use a tradition positively, and others may use that same tradition in a way that hinders.

What is a lifestyle? We can live a rugged lifestyle, a faithful lifestyle, a dangerous lifestyle, etc. etc. But a stewardship lifestyle? And how does a stewardship lifestyle intersect with the life of a disciple of Jesus Christ?

I wish to update the definition of stewardship as a lifestyle to a lifestyle that impacts all areas of our lives if we allow it. I intend to offer biblical and experiential evidence that challenges you to look at stewardship as a

God-designed lifestyle, a lifestyle of peace, joy, fulfillment, and provision. This updated stewardship lifestyle combines the life of faith with a life of compassion and action. It is a lifestyle of theology, philosophy, and hands-on experiences. It offers a full definition of being a disciple.

THE PROBLEM

What is the first thought that comes to mind if someone asks you the definition of stewardship? Do you relate to any of these people and their views?

One Sunday, after the pastor taught a message on stewardship, a group of congregants stand in the church foyer. A Builder-aged person says, "I sure wish the pastor didn't beg for money all of the time. It seems our church is only about asking for money. In my day, we didn't ask so much!"

A Baby Boomer agrees, "Yes, I think it is twice this year now that he taught on stewardship. I wonder how bad it is going to get. I give all I can, but there are other things that I think God can do with my money."

A younger member responds, "I have a young family and I just do not have enough extra to give to the church right now."

A long-time member complains, "Why does the pastor keep asking for money? I have been going here for twenty years and we always meet our budget. Our offering baskets always seem full when they are gathered up."

A visitor mutters, "This is my first time here and I'm not sure if I will come back. The first thing we heard was about money and why the church needs it. I am not sure I can trust a new organization that quickly."

A younger visitor says, "Just what I thought, heavy on fundraising, light on biblical content. We will visit a new church next week."

"Not having been to church before," says a visiting wife to her husband as they head toward their car, "it sure seems the people like to complain about money."

Conversations like these lead to key questions including: Is money the problem? Could it be that pastors and leaders have never learned how to teach stewardship correctly? Is stewardship about asking and budgets? Or is stewardship about the stewards' walk with Christ and how they view their time on earth? Is stewardship about a proper view of ownership and avoiding idols? Or is it about gathering bodies and buildings? Competent church leaders feel comfortable communicating biblical truths from church pulpits. They challenge, teach, inspire, and encourage their congregants. And yet, so many remain uncomfortable teaching about giving, stewardship, and money. These beliefs must be addressed in a straightforward manner with the bible as a guide. Leaders must not compromise in teaching people to be good stewards.

There are many Builder and Boomer-aged pastors who believe that after the Builder generation started new churches, ministries, and non-profit organizations following World War II, teaching stewardship in the church began its decline. Pastors receive little training on the subject in seminaries and theological schools. The result is that a secular fundraising profession now leads the way. As each new generation matures and begins volunteering and funding the church and parachurch ministries, they have no consistent teaching to guide them. The research shows little or no difference in motivation for giving between Christian or non-Christian donors.[1]

Because pastors have little to no formal training in this area, they resort to their own personal strategies or the latest technique. They tend to be uncomfortable with the subject, yet they know that it bears spiritual impact upon every one of their congregations.[2]

So the pastor reaches the foyer and begins discussions with the people in the congregation. He or she asks them, *"What did you think of my message? Was I too hard on the financial part?"*

The various congregants respond, *"No pastor, you were right on. That is the message that our church needs to hear. I just hope they were all listening."* The pastor leaves that day hoping the offering next week will meet budget needs, and without hearing the real conversation.

This simple illustration shows the inadequate under-standing of biblical stewardship. Churches face inade-quate teaching, wrong attitudes, and a lack of generosity in the church of Jesus Christ. This negatively impacts congregations, ministry organizations and the journey of stewards as they follow God.

---

[1] George Barna, "Churches Lose Financial Ground in 2000," The Barna Report, June 5, 2001, www.barna.org, accessed October 1, 2006.

[2] Gene A. Getz, *A Biblical Theology of Material Possessions*, Chicago: Moody Press, 1990, 11.

STEWARDSHIP AS A LIFESTYLE

A Christian's life is measured by many things. Scripture articulates some agreed-upon priorities: love, faith, fruit of the Spirit, honesty, turning the other cheek, taking care of widows and orphans, prayer, keeping the commandments, and sharing the gospel. Bruce Wilkinson suggests there is a time where Jesus Christ will ask those who believed in him what they have done with what he entrusted to them.[3] The apostle Paul refers to this judgment when he writes, *"not that I am looking for a gift, but I am looking for what may be credited to your account"* (Phil. 4:17 NIV). This suggests that each Christian has an eternal measurement of his or her stewardship here on earth and bears accountability.

Contemporary lifestyles offer good reasons to be critical. For instance, there is a clear distinction between North American lifestyles and lifestyles in impoverished countries.[4] The world continues evolving into have and have-not societies despite efforts to prevent it from happening.[5] It has been said one can tell someone's priorities by looking at their checkbook. Jacques Ellul states, *"Money has come to represent a certain type of 'spiritual' power in the contemporary society."*[6] This spiritual power controls how individuals think, spend, save, loan, or give money. It resides deep within each person and can be healthy or destructive. This power cannot easily be controlled. Some

---

[3] Bruce Wilkinson, *A Life God Rewards: Why Everything You Do Today Matters Forever,* Sisters, OR: Multnomah, 2002, 47.

[4] Robert Richards, *"The Economics Underlying Stewardship: Creation and Distribution of Wealth,"* Luther Seminary Stewardship Resource Database, http://www.luthersem.edu/stewardship/resource_detail.asp?resource_id=974, accessed November 28, 2007.

[5] Ibid.

[6] Jacques Ellul, *Violence: Reflections from a Christian Perspective,* trans. Cecilia Gaul Kings, New York: Seabury, 1969, under "The Fight of Faith," http://www.religion-online.org/showchapter.asp?title=573&C=715, accessed December 3, 2007.

stewardship writers have determined the only way not to be controlled by money is to give it away.[7]

It is important to think of stewardship as a comprehensive approach to life, including money, and to explore how often Jesus spoke of money and its hold on human life. God is concerned with what individuals do with their money. It is a major power in a person's life, and it can produce much good through wise earning, investment, saving, and giving. In contrast, it can produce idolatry, accumulation, greed, jealousy, divorce, and rejection of God as the owner of all creation. Through giving, the danger of this power can be held in check. Ellul writes, *"The law of money is the law of accumulation, of buying and selling. That is why the only way to overcome the 'spiritual' power of money, is to give our money away, thus desacralizing it and freeing us from its control."*[8]

A lifestyle of stewardship is more than a fundraising strategy. A strategy focuses on a teachable method for the church and other ministry organizations to communicate the raising of funds. A lifestyle, however, reflects a steward's relationship with God. This relationship between Creator and creation is holy and defined by actions. A stewardship lifestyle, then, reflects the individual's relationship with God and the choices they make in the context of that relationship.

Lifestyle Principle #1
We are encouraged to excel in the grace of giving, and seek to be generous on every occasion. The goal is not to be tithers, but to be known as generous. A disciple of Jesus Christ excels in generosity.

---

[7] Ibid.
[8] Ibid.

CHAPTER 2

A New Stewardship:
Relationship with the Owner

Wikipedia defines Stewardship as personal responsibility for taking care of another person's property or financial affairs or in religious orders taking care of finances.[9] To be a steward requires a relationship with the owner. To be a steward is to serve the master as in the parable of the talents.[10] The servants given either 10 or 5 talents seek to please the master by wise stewardship of their trust.

Why would a steward want to please the owner? Because they are in relationship. There must be a relationship for steward to be successful. Some might think this is a boss-slave relationship. Our relationship with Creator God is far from this. We have a relationship that is loving and generous. It is a relationship where the Owner is ready to give at every opportunity. The Owner's desire is for us to enjoy, use, and multiply what has been given. It is also the Owner's desire that, in turn, we become loving and generous in all areas of our lives.

In order to understand and live a stewardship as a lifestyle concept, we must first have a relationship with the Owner, our God. One must be in relationship with

[9] Wikipedia, accessed 5-20-09
[10] Matthew 25:14-30

the God of the Universe, the Creator of all, in order to be a steward. This is the same as it was for the original stewards of the garden—Adam and Eve. Their entire life was to be one of tending the wonderful garden. When they disobeyed God it was not because of poor gardening, it was because the relationship was broken.

So it is with each of us. In order to be a steward of the wonderful garden we call life, we must have a relationship with the Owner. It is through this relationship that we seek to grow in our stewardship lifestyle.

Lifestyle Principle #2
Stewardship is a lifestyle based on an understanding that we are in a relationship with the God who owns everything.

CHAPTER 3

The Journey of the Steward

Perhaps you heard the saying, "we are born with nothing, and we die with nothing." It might sound discouraging, but when you consider it in light of stewardship everything gets clarified!

For believers in Jesus Christ, each day is a journey with God. Stewardship becomes a daily aspect of decision-making and setting priorities. This is the disciples' daily journey—following Jesus while seeking to make wise stewardship decisions in all areas of life.

Stewardship decisions include how much time to spend in prayer and study God's Word, how much time to spend with spouses or children, how to share one's talents with a charity or a ministry, and how much to keep for one's self.

Principle #3
God is more concerned with the journey of the steward than with budgets and goals.

STEWARDSHIP AS TRANSFORMATION

The *Encarta World English Dictionary* defines transformation as *"a complete change, usually into something with an improved appearance or usefulness [and] the act or process of transforming somebody or something."*[11] Both definitions relate to the process of stewardship as transformation. As individuals are transformed into God's image they take on God's view of creation as well as their use of resources. This transformation is a lifelong process. Scott Rodin writes in *Revolution in Generosity*:

> *"The Christian life is a journey of transformation. From conversion to final glory we are called into a process of constant change, breaking away from the bondage of our old sinful nature and embracing the freedom of God's transforming grace. Our vocation involves dying to self and living for Christ. It requires us to lose a counterfeit life in order to find our true life. It is a shedding of our old nature and putting on Christ. It is a quest that promises nothing less than our re-creation as a new, holy and Christ-like child of God. While we will never attain the full end of this quest on this side of heaven, we are nonetheless compelled by the grace of God to enter unequivocally and sacrificially into the pursuit."*[12]

Transformation is central to the future of stewardship education and demands examination of the theological foundations of a relationship with Christ. Key questions include: What is the relationship that stewards have with God? How do stewards regard the possessions and resources God entrusts to them? How do these views and values influence stewards so they live differently and are transformed?

[11] *Encarta World English Dictionary*, 1999, s.v. "transformation."
[12] R. Scott Rodin, *Revolution in Generosity*, Chicago: Moody Press, 2008.

These questions have complicated answers. First, there is the spiritual response to transformation. Within each Christian is the power to be transformed by the Holy Spirit. For example, Hebrews asserts that individuals should desire deeper spiritual things rather than feeding on mere milk, implying that they are still spiritual children (Heb. 5:12-14). To be transformed is to become stewards for the God of creation and to see matters from an eternal perspective. In *The Treasure Principle* Randy Alcorn describes the eternal perspective as one of his six principles: *"seek the arrow, not the dot."*[13] This implies that Christians should focus on the journey, on the process of becoming more like Christ: more loving, more faithful, and more generous.

A second aspect of transformation is in the reality here on earth. To act as transformed stewards requires change in attitude and action. Transformed attitudes are demonstrated in the hearts of stewards and their reactions to those in need. Transformed spirits are sensitive to opportunities to be generous, rather than to accumulate. Transformed stewards are generous. They look to be examples of giving. They encourage others to be generous. They seek to be noticed only when it encourages others to give, rather than seeking personal acclaim. Their perspective is that giving is comprehensive, including money, time, a caring spirit, relationships, and every opportunity to be generous.

Transformation is a lifelong process, and transformational stewardship is of value in a stewards' journey. God is more concerned with a stewards' journey than with budgets and goals of congregations and ministries.

---

[13] Randy Alcorn, *The Treasure Principle: Discovering the Secret of Joyful Giving* , Sisters, OR: Multnomah Press, 2001, 49.

Principle #4
We must move from transactional giving to transformational stewardship.

Many in the stewardship profession are concerned with the movement toward transactional giving in nonprofit, church, and parachurch worlds. Giving to the local church has become a transaction that purchases something—a balanced budget, building renovations, equipment and activities for one's children, high tech worship services, access to someone's famous teaching, or a mission trip. This sort of teaching and modeling disconnects spiritual significance from giving. Giving as a purchase or transaction renders the act of giving self-serving and of little spiritual value. Generosity without spiritual significance increases desire to acquire things and distorts the value of earthly things. This desire conflicts with the scriptural witness. For example, Psalm 24:1 asserts, *"The earth is the Lord's and everything in it and all who dwell in it."* And the apostle Paul writes, *"Just as you excel in everything, in love, in faith, and in your earnestness for us, see also that you excel in this grace of giving"* (2 Cor. 8:7). Followers of Jesus (stewards) can seek to be excellent in giving and be known as people of love, faith, and generosity.

A third aspect of stewardship as transformation is the resulting change of focus. For many twenty-first century westerners, life is filled with goals and the desire to achieve a successful career, good marriage, and material possessions. When individuals achieve a certain status, they expect their income to grow. Income growth enables them to purchase more and accumulate possessions. A transformed steward, however, focuses on eternal things.

Jesus directs His followers to seek the things of the Kingdom, and many of his words challenge Christians to trust
in heavenly things.[14] Transformed stewards enjoy what
the Lord allows them to use during their lifetimes, but
they do not value them in the same way they value eternal things of God.

A transformed steward also has a change of heart. Transformed stewards give from internal motivation deep
within the spirit. Transformed stewards are transformed
by the renewing of their minds through their relationships with God in Jesus Christ. Their sense of God's
direction in how to give time, talent, and treasure moti-
vates their generosity, rather than coercion by the latest
marketing gimmick or transactional offering or fundraising challenge. Each time transformed stewards consider
an opportunity to be generous, they gain another chance
to communicate with the Creator, ask for wisdom, and
seek to be good stewards. Their prayers are rewarded
with God's peace and wisdom, and are multiplied in their
impact (Luke 6:38).

Principle #5
We in the local church and ministry organiza-
tions should put our emphasis where God places
emphasis: a relationship with the steward.

---

[14] For example: Matthew 6:20; Mark 8:34-38; Luke 12:16-21

STEWARDSHIP AS A LIFESTYLE:
FUTURE IMPACT ON THE CHURCH AND
PARACHURCH

The impact on the church of the future could be immense. Pastors could teach stewardship as part of the Christian life without guilt, shame, or fear. Church members could be generous as a way of life rather than just during a fund raising campaign. Young, emerging congregations could teach that a stewardship filter views the entirety of life as an opportunity to be a great steward.

The overall impact of teaching and learning about stewardship as a lifestyle could have a positive effect on seminaries, pastors, parachurch ministries, and followers of Jesus Christ. The newly created momentum could be a catalyst for the next generation of evangelism and leadership development as the body of Christ is grown and equipped.

For each disciple of Jesus who determines generosity priorities and seeks effective and strong ministries to give to, this fresh perspective could become a tool rather than a burden. Every disciple could seek to please God in every giving opportunity, rather than worrying about propping up an organizational budget or structure.

CHAPTER 4

God's Eternal Economic Equation

For a more comprehensive view of stewardship, the following statements present a logical path to follow in order to understand the stewardship journey. This *equation* is based on scriptural, logical, and theological foundations. These components combine in forming a holistic relationship with God that includes God's ownership, our stewardship, and our life with God after our time on earth. This equation does not yield the same result if any components are left out. All these components must be considered in the life of a steward.

a. *God is the source and owner of all and has a specific intention for it* - From the creation story to Jesus relating to his followers about the Kingdom of heaven, it is made clear that an all-powerful God created the universe and everything in it and intends a relationship with it. The Psalmist reminds us *"the earth is the Lord's and everything in it and all who dwell in it."*[15]

b. *God is the most generous giver* – At the foundation of any stewardship theology is a definition of generous. The steward looks to Creator God as the model

[15] Psalm 24:1

and example. The very gift of creation to man is the first recorded example of generosity.[16] There are many other biblical examples of God's continued generosity, but here we will deal with just one—the gift of God's Son, Jesus Christ.

A gift is given as a sign of affection or love. God's gift of Jesus is a perfect example of a demonstration of love, but it goes further. In this act of generosity is a painful separation between God who is Father and Son. This gift cost something. The gift was given through painful sacrifice. When Jesus died for the sins of humanity, he willingly experienced the pain of a broken relationship with God that we might have one. No greater love and generosity can be found than this.

c. *We are called to be stewards of creation* - Leonard Sweet brings an interesting perspective to the term stewardship. He proposes the use of the term trustee rather than steward. He states: *"Whereas 'steward-ship' has been stripped of all legal overtones and fiduciary consequences, postmoderns understand that the trustees of anything are the legal guardians of that organization or estate. They do not 'own' it, but they are legally accountable for its health and well-being."*[17] While I agree that in today's culture and time of organizational change the term trustee is appealing, I find it too much a change from the biblical focus. Neither does it help us educate people toward generosity. My view is that the true definition of steward and stewardship as more comprehensive would

---

[16] Genesis 1

[17] Sweet, Leonard, *Freely You Have Received, Freely Give*, 2005, www.leonardsweet.com.

receive a welcome in the postmodern church if properly positioned and taught.

We need to remember that we begin with gratitude. Theologian Catherin M. LaCugna wrote *"As we think about the acts of God on our behalf, our hearts respond with gratitude and we put our hands to the task of bearing a tangible witness to the redemption given in Christ. Then, as we think about living grateful lives, we realize that we are not really developing a theology of stewardship. Instead, we are discovering a theology which draws us directly into a life of stewardship."*[18]

d. *Our calling in stewardship is comprehensive* — The bible gives us examples of the wise stewardship of time, talent, treasure, but we can go much further in a holistic stewardship model. One example of the many additional arenas is the resource of touch. Our ability to touch someone's life with a handshake, a hug, or a pat on the back is something we give to another person. Another is our spiritual environment, not just how we build and care for it in nurturing our own soul, but how it provides benefit for others.

Another clear item from the bible is that the time, talent and treasure list is not a menu from which we choose. In other words, if you give time, it does not mean you now avoid giving treasure. This has been misused in many giving policies developed by churches and parachurch organizations. Some may believe that if you give time as a volunteer then you do not need to be a financial donor to the organization. While all gifts of time, leadership and volunteering are

[18] LaCugna, Catherine M., *God for Us: The Trinity and the Christian Life*, 1993, p. 377

appreciated, there is no measurement system set up in scripture to allow a gift of one type to cancel the need to grow in one's holistic stewardship.

Here is another example: natural resources. On the Acton Institute website, Lynn White is quoted as saying, *"Christianity is uniquely responsible for growing environmental problems."*[19] She also claims, *"Judeo-Christian religion was the world's most anthropocentric religion, blaming it for Western technologies' exploitative relationship with nature."*[20] It is a shame that some Christians shun responsibility when it comes to creation. If anything we should see creation's oversight as a key responsibility.

We seem to be increasing our awareness of this critical aspect of stewardship. If we are to be accountable for creation then we must begin considering the use of natural resources as part of our responsibility as stewards for the Creator. My research found 36 parachurch organizations working directly or indirectly with environmental issues. They want it known they are pro-environment and are adjusting their policies to be more sensitive to the wise use of natural resources.[21]

e.   *We manage different amounts and types of treasure* - Why is there poverty in the world? Why are some given riches and others experience poverty? The book of Deuteronomy says, *"Each of you must bring*

[19]*Theology and the Environment*, Acton Institute, 2006, www.acton.org/ppolicy/environment/theology.

[20] White, Jr., Lynn, *The Historical Roots of Our Ecologic Crisis*, Science Magazine, 1967.

[21] *Judeo-Christian Environmental Organizations*, Acton Institute, 2006, www.acton.org.

a gift in proportion to the way the Lord your God has blessed you."[22] This writing is about the Feast of the Tabernacles. Some might say it is an Old Testament concept, but the passage bears a closer look. The principle is that some will have different amounts of wealth than others, and from which they offer worship to God. This principle remains true throughout history and various cultures. A second principle links to this from the New Testament. The apostle Paul writes that we are to give based on what we have, not what someone else has.[23] Our unused capacities for generosity grow from our position in life, our talents, skills, etc. How we manage and grow our giving from these capacities is what we will be held accountable for.

f.   *We use everything for God's glory and Kingdom work* - In the parable of the owner and the servants[24], we can see the principle that generosity produces multiplication. We are expected to produce fruit and be missional in our life as a Christian. The Rev. C. W. Taylor states in an address to the General Convention of the Episcopal Church, *"Thus, stewardship is more than church support; it is the use of the gifts give to us to carry on Christ's work of reconciliation in the world. Therefore, the way we use or do not use resources to further unity and reconciliation in our homes, our communities, and our occupations is our stewardship."*[25] Our use of resources, including time, relationships, skills, and money, are to produce kingdom results. We do not

[22] Deuteronomy 16:17
[23] 2nd Corinthians 8:12
[24] Matthew 25: 14-30
[25] Taylor, Rev. C.W., *Stewardship is the Main Work of the Church*, 1988, www.resurrectionchurch/com/resources/stewardship.html

accumulate in hopes that one day we can be generous. Instead, we continually invest in Kingdom work by our generous acts.

g.   *We can enjoy God's gifts* - One important aspect of a steward's transformation is the ability to enjoy God's gifts. The bible is filled with examples of God's promises to meet our needs, that we can rely on God's provision, and that we can enjoy the time, health, relationships, and peace that God bestows upon us. We find God's promises to those who are generous in the Proverbs[26], and we find God's challenge to test and see his generosity throughout the bible.

One concern in the church is the teaching that God will make us rich and help us live in prosperity. I find that a key misunderstanding is in the interpretation of the word prosperity. To be prosperous in relationships, our career, and in our health would be a broad and good use of the word. The argument comes when use of the word shifts to material prosperity and becomes the goal—seeking material wealth and accumulating earthly goods. Those who are seriously considering the embrace of prosperity theology are wise to consider the definition cited by Wendell Smith in his book *Prosperity with a Purpose*. He writes that the only reason to seek material prosperity is to enhance and impact the Kingdom of God.[27]

Regardless, the sad truth is we neglected to teach God's desire for us to enjoy creation and God's provision because we fear a wrong interpretation. A transformational stewardship approach eliminates this misunderstanding. A steward who is transformed in their

[26] Proverbs 22:9; Proverbs 11:25
[27] Smith, Wendell, *Prosperity with a Purpose*, 2005, p.1-3

thinking about material provision God gives to us in creation will also seek this provision in all areas of life, and want to use it in all areas of life for the glory of God.

h. *We seek excellence in generosity* - Just as we are to be known as people of love and faith, we are to be people of generosity. Our generosity is not a minimal effort. Rather, we seek to excel in this form of grace.[28] To excel at something infers that we keep improving and become the best we can be. The apostle Paul expands on excelling in his second letter to the church at Corinth where he states, *"And God is able to make all grace abound to you, so that in all things at all times, having all that you need, you will abound in every good work."*[29] Later in the same chapter, Paul writes *"You will be made rich in every way so that you can be generous on every occasion."*[30] Paul purposefully uses the terms *all* and *every* to be comprehensive. As transformed stewards we seek excellence in our generosity at all times and in every way. This does not mean we have to donate to every charity or ministry that asks for assistance, but it does mean we are ready for God's Spirit to move us to generosity of our time, talent, treasure, touch, environment, relationships until all facets of life are involved .

i. *God watches and keeps account of our stewardship* – Paul challenges the church in Philippi with these words, *"not that I am looking for a gift, but I am looking for what may be credited to your account."*[31]

[28] 2nd Corinthians 8:7
[29] 2nd Corinthians 9:8
[30] 2nd Corinthians 9:11
[31] Philippians 4:17

What does Paul mean by *account*? Upon closer look at Jesus' parables, we see him repeatedly referring to a master who watches what the servants do. We also find a passage in Luke's gospel, *"to whom much is given, much will be required."*[32] That verse reminds us that God invests in each of us expecting a return. Just as any owner would of any investment, God uses us to multiply and make an eternal impact on this world. Reward flows accordingly.[33]

j. *God promises blessings to those who are generous* – These promises to those who are generous deserve more attention. Receiving these blessings begins with becoming generous. Much like the Israelites escaping the Egyptians at the Red Sea, we need to take a step of faith in giving before the waters divide. This can be attributed to a first fruits principle established in Deuteronomy 26, exhorted in the book of Malachi and reinforced in the gospel of Luke. [34] When a faithful steward steps out and gives, God promises to be faithful and give them an abundant response. These blessings will be more than we would normally expect. An example: in Douglas Lawson's research, he finds evidence that generosity and giving produces a longer, healthier life.[35]

k. *One day God will reward us according to our wise stewardship* – Some scholars and pastors believe that the idea of working for an eternal reward creates a self-centered approach to giving. Others think that these eternal rewards are a key behavior of a transformed steward. Randy Alcorn writes, *"You cannot*

---

[32] Luke 12:48b

[33] Luke 12:42-44

[34] Deuteronomy 26; Malachi 3; Luke 6:38

[35] Lawson, Douglas M., *Give to Live*, Alti Publishing, 1998, p.20

take it with you, but you can send it on ahead."[36] Transformed stewards have an eternal viewpoint of all of life, especially in regards to stewardship. This final step in the eternal equation is that God keeps an account of our spiritual investments of generosity and will be saves it for us for this life and the life to come. Jesus directed us to seek first the Kingdom of Heaven and things of eternal value, because everything else decays and rots. These things of eternal value never decay. They will be there for us to enjoy with the Creator of all.

This eternal economic equation is completed when the steward (the created) is returned to the Creator. There we face God and give account for what was entrusted to us. We will look at the entirety of life, then, thus making it important to get started with this equation now.

[36] Alcorn, Randy, *The Treasure Principle*, Multnomah Press, 2001, p. 17

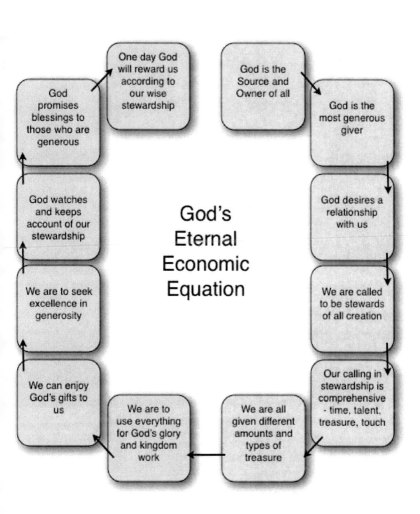

CHAPTER 5

A Lifestyle of Generosity, Being a Disciple

As mentioned as this book opened, living a stewards' lifestyle is a series of bold choices. When we choose to live a lifestyle of following God, we make a choice to follow in the footsteps of our example, Jesus. While Jesus did not face the many electronic, technical and cultural issues of our time, his lifestyle of generosity can still be observed and followed.

Being a disciple of Jesus Christ is a daily following of him and his ways. In Luke's gospel a follower of Jesus is instructed to take up his cross and follow Jesus (Luke 9:23). Taking up the cross is choosing to follow Jesus' teachings rather than those of the world. Stewardship decisions follow this same journey throughout each day. This is not one-time giving of a financial gift or being kind to someone on occasion. It is cultivating a daily concern to use one's life, talents and resources in the world in which one lives, bringing honor and glory to God.

SECTION TWO

Application of a
Stewardship Lifestyle

CHAPTER 6

A Lifestyle: Stewardship of Your Time

We know time is a valuable commodity. We have so much to do and accomplish that our days become filled with things that burn up time. Time is not reproducible. We cannot add more days or make our days longer. Once time is used it is gone.

We are sobered when we realize God holds us accountable for our use of time as a steward under divine ownership. We think of the time we wasted and remained unconcerned about its misuse or loss.

Here are some time stewardship considerations:

1. Do you give time to regular conversation with God?

2. What quantity of time is given to your spouse and children?

3. Can you identify a quantity of time you are available for your neighbor?

4. How does this compare to the time given to TV, sports, hobbies, internet, etc.?

Hobbies, distractions, TV, etc. are not necessarily harmful, but we must ask the stewardship question. Do you consume your time for these items instead of for your relationship with God, family and neighbor?

CHAPTER 7

A Lifestyle: Stewardship of Your Talent

Each of us receives talent from Creator God. Do you believe that? We might sometimes feel we have nothing to offer or give. Only *up front* people have real talent. Or we think of music and movie people as the ones with talent. This is so not true. In the book of Ephesians, the apostle Paul writes, "*It was he who gave some to be apostles, some to be prophets, some to be evangelists, and some to be pastors and teachers, 12to prepare God's people for works of service, so that the body of Christ may be built up 13until we all reach unity in the faith and in the knowledge of the Son of God and become mature, attaining to the whole measure of the fullness of Christ.*" (Ephesians 4:11-13) You may have a talent for helping those in need. You may have a talent to fix cars, create paintings or create wonderful meals. The concept is not to look just at obvious talents that people see, but rather the talents that God gave you to share with the body of Christ.

Reflect on these questions as a steward of your talents:

1. What talents did God give you?

2. How can you/do you steward those talents with your family?

3. How can you/do you steward those talents with your local church?

4. How can you/do you steward those talents in your local community?

Sharing talent can be scary at first. Remember, however, your talents are entrusted to you by God, and they are not to go to waste. God will ask you some day why you did or did not use the talents given you for his glory. What answer will you give?

CHAPTER 8

A Lifestyle:
Stewardship of Your Treasure

We know many if not all churches and pastors and leaders of nonprofit ministries start here, often adding to the criticism that asks, *"Why is the church always teaching about or asking for money?"* From a strictly biblical perspective, the answer is because it is their responsibility to teach the truth about how God sees money, its uses, and how the follow of Jesus should think about, earn, save, loan, and give money as part of their relationship with Jesus.

Jesus spoke more about money than heaven and hell combined when he was with his disciples. Why? I think it is because Jesus knew how money could corrupt us, distract us, and move us away from God. A key illustration of this harm is how divorce so often involves disputes regarding money.[37] Jesus warns us that it is easier for a camel to go through the eye of a needle than for a rich man to enter the kingdom of heaven. Why? Because the rich man grows fond of his riches and they govern his life.

---

[37]   http://economix.blogs.nytimes.com/2009/12/07/money-fights-predict-divorce-rates/, accessed August 22, 2012.

Jesus also warns us that we cannot serve the two masters: God and mammon. Why? Because God is a jealous God and will not share our loyalties. If we begin to love money, we will be controlled by money, and God will not share the leftovers.

Our recent recession of 2008-2012 is an example of this competition, especially for church leadership. A good number of churches laid off or cut salaries of pastors and church staff—even before they described the situation and asked their congregations to give more. They assumed their people had given all they could and therefore did not ask. And yet, a research project entitled State of the Plate[38] show that while 38% of churches saw giving drop, 62% of churches found that giving met or exceeded goals. Their reasons: teaching stewardship from the pulpit and offering classes in stewardship and finances.

When the body of Christ learns what scripture really has to say about generosity and money, it is a freeing experience. God does not want us to be bound by money, but to use it as a tool to extend God's work in our world. And yet, because money has a spiritual component, it also serves as a tool to confuse and bind us to things of this world.

[38] Kluth, Rev. Brian, *State of the Plate*, Maximum Generosity, 2009, 2010.

CHAPTER 9

A Lifestyle:
Stewardship of Your Relationships

My wife shared reminded me one day when I was quite grouchy that only relationships were important to God. Only relationships go with us to heaven. I have given that a lot of thought and figure that although I might live on the streets of gold in heaven, due to my lack of focus on relationships it might be out in the woods in a little camper! I had better get serious about my stewardship of relationships while I still have time.

God created us for relationship, first with him, then with what has been created. Relationships are hard to understand, create, define, and sustain. Yet, God values them so much he gave his Son so we could be reconnected to God in a spiritual and real relationship.

How much value do we place in the relationship we have with our spouse? Our children? Our neighbor? Our co-workers? Our neighbor on the bus, train, and airplane? As I travel by air a great deal this is a tough one for me. Many times I do not want to enter into relationship with the people around me in the airplane, especially if they have a child with them. This attitude exposes my priorities and selfishness. If it is in giving that I find Jesus showing through me, when I offer my seat so a couple can sit together I am blessing them and receive a blessing myself.

As parents, we are wise stewards for our children by guiding and teaching, but sometimes also by saying nothing so that the learning comes in their timing. This is just one example of sensitivity to our stewardship responsibility within relationships that God can help us cultivate.

Some items to consider regarding relational stewardship:

1.   What is the status of your family relationships?

2.   What is the status your relationships in your congregation?

3.   What is the status of your community and work relationships?

4.   What is the status of your relationship with God?

5.   How might you improve your stewardship within any of these relationships?

CHAPTER 10

A Lifestyle:
Stewardship of Your Priorities

When we become retrospective over our lives and think our decision-making experiences, we might say, *"If I knew then what I know now, I would have made a wiser choice."* What do we learn over time? What do we acquire that allows us to make better choices in life?

I suggest it is wisdom with our priorities, our stewardship of them. We make many decisions every day. It might be how much time we give to something, how much money we spend or save, or even how we invest in our families or other relationships.

In each of these situations we determine our priorities. We say *this* is more important than *that*. These priorities shape our lives behind the scenes. We might think about priorities openly when we make decisions, but our decisions are often influenced by priorities shaped previously across a lifetime of decisions, and which operate behind the scenes.

Think about a recent day and the decisions you made. How were they influenced by your priorities? These priorities were created and refined over your lifetime based on your experiences and learning. You might think something was important when you were young, and now it hardly seems to matter. Refining and updating priorities is an important part of our stewardship. We should learn and grow wiser through life, adjusting our priorities as wise stewardship.

Here are some appropriate reflection questions on the subject:

1.   What is a priority you had when you were young but no longer have?

2.   Why did your priority change?

3.   What are some priorities you have now you did not have previously?

4.   How might you exercise a better stewardship of your priorities?

CHAPTER 11

A Lifestyle:
Stewardship of Your World

Did God tell us to use up (consume) our world, or to be stewards of our world? It is a question worth pondering. I suggest when God told humans to tend the garden, God meant they should be stewards rather than use it up at will. From a disciple's viewpoint, living as a steward involves attention to all of the resources God gives us in this world. It includes all of creation and demands that each of us are aware of those things we can do to be wise stewards.

I remember the 1960's when it became illegal to litter along the roads. It seems crazy now, but back then many thought littering was no big deal. Yet, as more people traveled and roads were built everywhere, it became apparent that throwing everything out the window was not good stewardship. Littering became illegal, but it took many years to change people's viewpoints and practice. Now littering or dumping trash along the road is seen as shameful. What changed? Was it the law alone, or a collective and deeper understanding of our stewardship?

As we become more aware of our responsibility to steward all resources in our world, we are better and wiser disciples of Jesus.

Some items to consider:

1. Do you see all trees, land, and water as gifts from God?

2. Do you see fish, birds, and mammals as gifts from God?

3. How do you/will you include being a steward of creation in your lifestyle?

4. How do you view the creation account in Genesis 1 and our privilege to tend and steward?

CHAPTER 12

A Lifestyle: Stewardship of Your Faith

Did you ever think that in order to be a true steward you must have a relationship with the owner? As we read the parables of the Talents, we see the workers wanting to please the owner. They strive to please him and their reward is based on their wise multiplication of a principle investment they are given. Wise stewardship earns them a reward. So it is with us and God.

Why desire to be a good steward? Are you in relationship with the Creator of the universe? Are you in relationship with Jesus who became flesh and died to be the final sacrifice for sin? It is this relationship with the owner that compels us to be good stewards. It is this relationship that guides our lives as followers of Jesus.

The apostle Paul provides an example and challenges us to be disciples who are obedient to the Word of God ready to share our faith.[39] Are you ready to share the Gospel of Jesus Christ at each opportunity?

Stewardship of faith is also a trust God gives us. Saint Francis of Assisi is credited with teaching us to *"be ready to share the Gospel on all occasions, and if necessary use*

---

[39] Colossians 1:28

words." I learn from this that we are to be walking and talking examples of the Jesus we follow. We are entrusted with God's eternal message of salvation for the world. And like most things God has entrusted to us, God will ultimately host a moment for our accountability. Our entire stewardship will be on display, including our stewardship of the gospel.

Another component of our faith is our consistent reflection on God's word and our conversation with God in prayer. Do I scan the internet for news over reading God's word? Do I talk to God and worship him, or prefer the TV instead? While these choices might seem contrived, I believe we are accountable for these stewardship decisions in our life of faith.

Consider these questions:

1. Do I view my life of faith as something I should steward?

2. Do I live my life understanding that how others view me is how they might also view Jesus, and that I bear responsibility for how their view is shaped?

3. What is one recent action I took to strengthen the stewardship of my faith? How is it working?

SECTION THREE

The Steward As Disciple

CHAPTER 13

Walking with God:
A Stewardship Lifestyle as a Disciple

Discipleship is a daily walk with Jesus. It is EVERY day, not just a day set aside as Sabbath. It is viewing each day and every moment within it as a gift from God. A disciple holds to a set of values that guides them in their daily following of Jesus. A life of total stewardship becomes a guidebook for the disciple. When we understand, view, and live by stewardship principles we have a guide for all decisions in life.

A daily walk with God is not easy. It takes discipline to abide in Christ while we read God's word and seek to follow God's commands. How does the disciple stay a true and thorough follower every day? I believe it is by looking at life through a stewardship filter. A stewardship filter is what God gives us to guide and direct our lives as disciples.

If you review these short chapters on stewardship you will see that being a disciple (which actually means being a follower) means you consider all resources, talents, priorities, and relationships around you. You ask yourself, *"How would God want me to steward this time or this resource or this situation?"* You develop a process of

tuning in to the Holy Spirit and discerning how to pro-
ceed. This communication with God about stewardship
decisions brings you closer to God, serving and pleasing
him. And after all, isn't that what a relationship with God
is all about?

Acknowledgments

As always a book cannot be written and produced by one person. Over the past few years many people had input in my life that impacted the writing of this book. I am thankful to Mark and Lorie Vincent and the folks at Design Group International for their support, editing, and belief in this project.

My thanks to my friends at The Center in Edmonds, WA. They were there when I needed them. And thanks to Richard Maxwell, my wise counselor who always tells me the truth with grace and the Word.

My faithful friend Leon Negen of Hope Ministries in Des Moines, IA has been a steady influence and counsel through the years. We depend one each other and it makes a difference.

Finally, to my wife Susan, my best and sometimes only friend. You are my delight in life. Thank you.

And to God, may this be pleasing to you.

BIBLIOGRAPHY

Alcorn, Randy, *Money, Possessions, and Eternity,* Carol Stream, IL: Tyndale, 2003.

_____, *The Treasure Principle: Discovering the Secret of Joyful Giving,* Sisters, OR: Multnomah, 2001.

Barna, George, *The Barna Update,* 2002, The Barna Group, http://www.barna.org.

_____, *Churches Lose Financial Ground in 2000,* The Barna Group, http://www.barna.org.

_____, *House Churches Are More Satisfying to Attenders Than Are Conventional Churches,* The Barna Group. http://www.barna.org.

_____, *How to Increase Giving in Your Local Church,* Ventura, CA: Regal, 1997.

_____, *Revolution,* Wheaton, IL: Tyndale, 2005.

Block, Peter, *Stewardship: Choosing Service over Self-Interest,* San Francisco: Berrett-Koehler, 1993.

Blomberg, Craig L. Heart, *Soul, and Money: A Christian View of Possessions,* Joplin, MO: College Press, 2000.

_____, *Neither Poverty nor Riches: A Biblical Theology of Material Possessions*, Grand Rapids, MI: William B. Eerdmans, 1999.

Bremner, Robert H, *Giving*, New Brunswick, NJ: Transaction, 1994.

Callahan, Kennon L, *Giving and Stewardship in an Effective Church: A Guide for Every Member*, San Francisco: Jossey-Bass, 1997.

Champlin, Joseph M, *Grateful Caretakers of God's Many Gifts: A Parish Manual to Foster the Sharing of Time, Talent, and Treasure*, Collegeville, MN: Liturgical Press, 2002.

_____, *A Way of Life: Four Faith-Sharing Sessions About Sacrificial Giving, Stewardship, and Grateful Caretaking*, Collegeville, MN: Liturgical Press, 2004.

Christian and Missionary Alliance. *Theology of Stewardship: An Executive Summary,* Christian and Missionary Alliance. http://www.cmalliance.org/search/?query=Theology%20of%20Stewardship.

Christian Community Foundation, http://www.thefoundations.org

Christian Leadership Alliance, http://www.christianleadershipalliance.org.

_____, *Biblical Principles of Stewardship and Fundraising,* Christian Stewardship Association. http://www.stewardship.org/resources/Fund_Articles/principles-fundraising.html.

_____, 2007 *Steward Leadership Institute: Development,* Christian Stewardship Association. http://www.stewardship.org/events/Institute/ 2007/index_old.html.

Commission on Stewardship and Development, *Report to the General Convention, Episcopal Church Report,* 2005, 279-383.

Crown Financial Ministries, http://www.crown.org.

Delloff, Linda Marie, *Beyond Stewardship: A Theology of Nature,* The Lutheran, 2006, http://www.webofcreation.org/Manuals/krause/ foreword.html.

Doudera, Ralph, *Wealth Conundrum*, Atlanta, GA: Christian Wealth, 2005.

Durall, Michael, *Creating Congregations of Generous People: Money, Faith, and Lifestyle Series*, Herndon, VA: The Alban Institute, 1999.

Ecumenical Stewardship Center, http://www.stewardshipresources.org.

Ellul, Jacques, *The Fight of Faith,* in Violence: Reflections from a Christian Perspective, Translated by Cecilia Gaul Kings, New York: Seabury, 1969, http://www.religion-online.org/showchapter.asp?title=573&C=715.

Episcopal Church of the Resurrection, http://www. resurrectionchurch.com.

Eternal Perspective Ministries, http://www.epm.org.

Frank, John R, *The Ministry of Development: An Introduction to the Strategies for Successful Christian Ministry,* 2nd ed, Design Group International, 2010.

Generous Giving, http://www.generousgiving.org

Getz, Gene A, *A Biblical Theology of Material Possessions,* Chicago: Moody Press, 1990.

_____, *Real Prosperity: Biblical Principles and Material Possessions,* Chicago: Moody Press, 1990.

The Good Steward, http://www.thegoodsteward.com

Grimm, Eugene, *Generous People,* Edited by Herb Miller. Nashville, TN: Abingdon Press, 1992.

Grissen, Lillian V, *Firstfruits: Managing the Master's Money,* 2nd ed, Orland Park, IL: Barnabas Foundation, 1992.

Guinness, Os, *Doing Well and Doing Good,* Colorado Springs: NavPress, 2001.

Hall, Douglas John, *The Steward: A Biblical Symbol Come of Age,* Grand Rapids, MI: William B. Eerdmans, 1990.

Hybels, Bill, *The Volunteer Revolution*, Grand Rapids, MI: Zondervan, 2004.

Jeavons, Thomas H., and Rebekah Burch Basinger, *Growing Givers' Hearts: Treating Fundraising as a Ministry*, San Francisco: Jossey-Bass, 2000.

Kelly, Russell Earl, *Should the Church Teach Tithing?* New York: Writers Club Press, 2000.

Kluth, Brian, *Biblical Resources and Speaking Ministry to Increase Giving*, Maximum Generosity, http://www.kluth.org

Lawson, Douglas M, *Give to Live: How Giving Can Change Your Life*, La Jolla, CA: ALTI, 1991.

Levan, Christopher. *Living in the Maybe: A Steward Confronts the Spirit of Fundamentalism*, Grand Rapids, MI: William B. Eerdmans, 1998.

MacDonald, Gordon, *Secrets of the Generous Life*, Wheaton, IL: Tyndale, 2002.

Michael, S. H, *We're in the Money!* Christianity Today, 44, no. 7, 2000.

Miller, Herb, Full Disclosure: *Everything the Bible Says About Financial Giving,* Nashville, TN: Discipleship Resources, 2003.

Money for Ministry, http://www.moneyforministry.com.

North, Gary, *Tithing and the Church*, Tyler, TX: Institute for Christian Economics, 1994.

O'Hurley-Pitts, Michael, *The Passionate Steward: Recovering Christian Stewardship from Secular Fundraising*, Toronto: St. Brigid Press, 2002.

Ortberg, John, Laurie Pederson, and Judson Poling, *Giving: Unlocking the Heart of Good Stewardship*, Grand Rapids, MI: Zondervan, 2000.

Oster, Merrill J., and Mike Hamel, *Giving Back: Using Your Influence to Create Social Change*, Colorado Springs: NavPress, 2003.

Perkins, John, H, *Practical Theology: What Will it Become,* Christian Century, February 1-8, 1984.

Piper, John, *Money: The Currency of Christian Hedonism*, Vol. 1. Chattanooga, TN: Generous Giving, 2003.

Presbyterian Church USA, *Living Grateful Lives: Stewardship Theology in Our Time,* Presbyterian Church USA http://www.secondpres.info/about2pc/Stewardship.htm

Ramp, Stephen, *Carnal Giving vs. Biblical Stewardship,* The Clergy Journal, 2003, 15-16.

Reid, David R, *Stewardship Theology,* The Living Pulpit, July-September 2006, http://www.pulpit.org/articles/StewardshipTheology.asp.

Reumann, John, *Stewardship and the Economy of God*, Grand Rapids, MI: William B. Eerdmans, 1992.

Rockwell, Bruce, *Parish Stewardship Program: My Theology of Stewardship,* Episcopal Diocese of Western Massachusetts, http://www.diocesewma.org/resources/parishstew.html.

Rodin, Scott, *Stewards in the Kingdom: A Theology of Life in All Its Fullness,* Downers Grove, IL: Inter-Varsity Press, 2000.

_____ and Gary Hoag, *The Sower*, 2010.

Roost, Charles, Taking Hold of Life, Steward to Steward, Winter 2007, 2.

_____ and Ben Ingebretson. *All the Gold Is Mine,* Growing in the Grace of Giving Foundational Papers, no. 2. Grand Rapids, MI: International Steward for the Freedom Foundation, 2003.

Schwarzentraub, Betsy, *Afire with God: Becoming Spirited Stewards,* Nashville, TN: Discipleship Resources, 2000.

Smith, Wendell, and Oral Roberts, *Prosperity with a Purpose*, Kirkland, WA: The City Church Press, 2005.

Stanley, Andy, *Fields of Gold*, Carol Stream, IL: Tyndale, 2004.

_____, *Sowing Seeds of Generosity,* Message Given at Generous Giving Conference, Generous Giving, http://www.generousgiving.org.

Stott, John R.W, *Generous Giving,* Generous Giving 1, no. 15, 2003, 1.

Strait, C. Neal, *Stewardship Is More Than Time, Talent, and Things*, Kansas City, MO: Beacon Hill Press, 1993.

Sweet, Leonard ed, *The Church in Emerging Culture: Five Perspectives*, Grand Rapids, MI: Zondervan, 2003.

_____, *Freely You Have Received, Freely Give,* 2005, http://www.leonardsweet.com/includes/ShowSweetenedArticlesasp?articleID=91.

Tamasy, Robert J, *The Handout, Andy Stanley Gave It Away,* Life@Work, no. 3, 2000, 48.

Taylor, C. W, *Stewardship is the Main Work of the Church*, Episcopal Church of the Resurrection, http://www.resurrectionchurch.com/resources/stewardship.html.

Towner, Dick, *10 Questions for Dick Towner of Willow Creek Association*, Christian Stewardship Association, http://www.stewardship.org/resources/ Fund_Articles/ towner_art.html.

_____, *More Good $ense,* November 2006, Willow Creek Association. www.goodsenseministry.com/newsletter.

United States Conference of Catholic Bishops Ad Hoc Committee on Stewardship, *Stewardship: A Disciple's Response: A Pastoral Letter on Stewardship*, Washington, D.C.: Conference of Catholic Bishops, 2002.

Vincent, Mark L. A Christian View of Money: Celebrating God's Generosity, 3rd ed, Wipf and Stock, 2007.

_____, *Speaking About Money: Reducing the Tension*, Scottdale, PA: Herald Press, 2001.

Warren, Rick, *Biblical Generosity, Message Given at Generous Giving Conference,* Generous Giving. http://www.generousgiving.org (accessed August 15, 2006).

Watley, William D, *Bring the Full Tithe: Sermons on the Grace of Giving*, Valley Forge, PA: Judson Press, 1995.

Web of Creation, http://www.webofcreation.org.

Weiss, Daniel, *The History of Economic Dependence: The Need to Rethink Prevailing Approaches to Missions,* International Steward, 2005, 1-2.

Wiersbe, Warren W, *Classic Sermons on Stewardship,* Grand Rapids, MI: Kregel, 1999.

Wilkinson, Bruce, *A Life God Rewards: Why Everything You Do Today Matters Forever,* Sisters, OR: Multnomah, 2002.

Willmer, Wesley K, ed, *Revolution in Generosity: Transforming Stewards to Be Rich Toward God,* Chicago, IL, Moody, 2008.

Willmer, Wesley K, J. David Schmidt, and Martyn Smith, *The Prospering Parachurch: Enlarging the Boundaries of God's Kingdom,* San Francisco: Jossey-Bass, 1998.

Willmer, Wesley K, and Martyn Smith, *God and Your Stuff: The Vital Link between Your Possessions and Your Soul,* Colorado Springs: NavPress, 2002.

Wuthnow, Robert, and Virginia A. Hodgkinson, *Faith and Philanthropy in America: Exploring the Role of Religion in America's Voluntary Sector,* San Francisco: Jossey-Bass, 1990.

Dr. John R. Frank, CFRE, CCNL

Speaker – Trainer - Author

John Frank is passionate about stewardship. He studies, teaches, and consults on stewardship and believes it is the key to a holistic approach to life for individuals and organizations. www.TheFrankGroup.us

A nationally and internationally recognized speaker and teacher, John's expertise includes stewardship, leadership, nonprofit organizations, as well as biblical training in various topics. He speaks with churches, ministry leadership, boards, and retreats.

His life experience includes ministry to 24 countries, pastor of worship, teaching stewardship in third world countries, evangelist outreaches behind the Iron Curtain, as well as church leadership. He has consulted with and provided training for many ministries ranging from start-ups to those with $100 million annual budgets.

He has authored articles numerous on stewardship, development and leadership and his first book "The Ministry of Development" was published in 1996 and reprinted in 2010. His second book, "The Monthly Partner" was published in 2005. He is a contributing author to "Revolution in Generosity" as well as having contributed to "From Soup & a Sermon to Mega-Mission, A Guide to Financing Rescue Missions" and two chapters in "In the Trenches, You and Your Nonprofit".

He is the Founder/Director of the Stewardship Summit, a meeting to bring those interested in the research, writing, teaching, and learning about stewardship in the church and parachurch together. www.stewardshipsummit.org

CPSIA information can be obtained at www.ICGtesting.com
Printed in the USA
LVOW050039270213

321846LV00001B/4/P

9 781457 515767